Handwriting
practice made fun

jokes, riddles, stories, & more!

- - - - - - - - - - -

Growing Minds
PRESS

Visit Us Online

Download Free Printables

growingmindspress.wixsite.com/home

Follow us on social media:

Copyright © 2022 Growing Minds Press

All rights reserved. No part of this publication may be reproduced, stored in a retrieval system or transmitted in any form or by any means, electronic, mechanical, photocopying, recording or otherwise, without prior permission of the publisher, except as permitted by U.S. copyright law.

Our Print Handwriting Program

Our print handwriting program is a comprehensive series of five books that includes instructional workbooks with corresponding animated YouTube videos, practice workbooks, and free resources on our website. We use a systematic approach that is outlined on the next few pages.

Book #1: Pre-writing Practice Made Fun: Preschool Writing Activities
Grades: Preschool – Pre-Kindergarten (ages 3-5)

Pre-writing and Fine Motor Skills
With this workbook, preschoolers can practice pre-writing strokes in preparation for letter and number formation. We have intentionally omitted lowercase letters in order to maintain a developmentally appropriate focus on pre-writing strokes, uppercase letters, and numbers. As developing fine motor skills is critical for handwriting success, we provide free resources on our website to assist you in fostering this important area of your child's development. We recommend using small golf size pencils or crayons broken in half to help your preschooler with their grasp while they enjoy this workbook.

Book #2: Handwriting Practice Made Fun: Focus on Formation
Grades: Pre-Kindergarten – 1st Grade (ages 4-7)

A Solid Foundation in Handwriting
Learning letter and number formation is a critical component for a solid foundation in handwriting. This workbook provides important step-by-step instruction presented in a stroke-based teaching order built on developmental progression. We focus on correct handwriting formation so that learners can eventually write letters and numbers with automaticity. We also encourage you to continue using the free and fun fine motor activities on our website for a positive impact on your child's handwriting development.

Our Print Handwriting Program

Animated Lesson Videos

A unique and valuable part of our program is our free animated lesson videos featuring our lovable joke-telling character, Funny Bunny Frankie. These videos bring handwriting to life by demonstrating how each letter and number is formed using simple movements that your child can easily understand. Together, this workbook and the corresponding videos provide a multi-sensory approach that will appeal to all learners.

Letter Reversals or Dyslexia?

We also address the common problem of letter reversals. Many parents believe when they see their child writing letters backwards or upside down that it is indicative of dyslexia. This is a misconception. It is normal for children under the age of 8 to write letters in reverse. With our program, we address letter reversals early, which can prevent the issue from starting or continuing. If your child is age 8 or older and continues to write letters in reverse after specifically addressing letter reversals, then we recommend consulting a professional as it may or may not be related to dyslexia.

Book #3: Handwriting Practice Made Fun: Focus on Size and Placement
Grades: 1st Grade – 3rd Grade (ages 6-9)

Handwriting Size and Placement

The next step in our handwriting program teaches your child how to correctly size and place letters and numbers on handwriting lines. Being aware of how to effectively use the handwriting lines will help your learner improve their handwriting skills. We continue our stroke-based teaching order to reinforce handwriting formation while they build the next progression of skills.

Our Print Handwriting Program

Animated Videos

Our lovable joke-telling friend Funny Bunny Frankie is back in this workbook and in animated videos to introduce his friends the Alpha Buddies. Together they will show your learner how to identify where each letter and number belong on the handwriting lines. These fun videos teach your child the purpose of each line and will keep them engaged while they focus on the size and placement of their handwriting.

Book #4: Handwriting Practice Made Fun: Silly Sentences
Grades: 1st Grade – 4th Grade (ages 6-10)

Letter and Sentence Handwriting Practice

The next workbook in our handwriting series provides letter and sentence practice using sight words. Students will roll a die to select words from lists that will help them build silly sentences. They will copy their silly sentence on handwriting lines and perform self-checks to ensure proper sentence formation. We use a focus letter with each worksheet to provide ample letter practice while also practicing handwriting with sentences. If your child enjoys being silly, they'll enjoy practicing handwriting with this silly and fun workbook.

Book #5: Handwriting Practice Made Fun: Jokes, Riddles, Stories, and More!
Grades: 2nd Grade – 4th Grade (ages 7-10)

Sentence Handwriting Practice

This handwriting practice workbook has a variety of fun activities for tracing and copying sentences. Using jokes, riddles, silly stories, fun facts, and decoding learners will practice handwriting in a fun and engaging way. If your child needs any review, they can watch the appropriate videos from our YouTube channel.

Which Book Should I Choose?

We have provided general placement guidelines by grade and age. Consider your child's skill level and needs when making your decision.

Preschool (ages 3-4)

> #1: Pre-Writing Practice Made Fun: Preschool Writing Activities

Pre-Kindergarten (ages 4-5)

> #1: Pre-Writing Practice Made Fun: Preschool Writing Activities
> OR
> #2: Handwriting Practice Made Fun: Focus on Formation

If you check one or more of the boxes below, choose Book #1. If not, choose Book #2

- ❏ My child has had little or no prior pre-writing strokes practice (vertical lines, horizontal lines, circle, cross, diagonal lines, square, X, and triangle)
- ❏ My child needs more pre-writing stokes practice
- ❏ My child has difficulty with some of the pre-writing strokes

Which Book Should I Choose?

Kindergarten (ages 5-6)

#2: Handwriting Practice Made Fun: Focus on Formation

1st Grade (ages 6-7)

#2: Handwriting Practice Made Fun: Focus on Formation
OR
#3: Handwriting Practice Made Fun: Focus on Size and Placement
OR
#4: Handwriting Practice Made Fun: Silly Sentences

- ❏ My child needs more help to correctly form letters and numbers (Choose Book #2)
- ❏ My child forms letters and numbers correctly (Choose Book #3)
- ❏ My child has finished Book #3 (Choose Book #4)

Which Book Should I Choose?

2nd Grade – 3rd Grade (ages 7-9)

> #3: Handwriting Practice Made Fun: Focus on Size and Placement
> OR
> #4: Handwriting Practice Made Fun: Silly Sentences
> OR
> #5: Handwriting Practice Made Fun: Jokes, Riddles, Stories, and More!

- ☐ My child needs help to correctly form some letters or numbers (Choose Book #3)
- ☐ My child needs help to place some letters or numbers correctly on handwriting lines (Choose Book #3)
- ☐ My child needs both letter and sentence handwriting practice (Choose Book #4)
- ☐ My child needs just handwriting practice with sentences (Choose Book #5)

4th Grade (ages 9-10)

> #4: Handwriting Practice Made Fun: Silly Sentences
> OR
> #5: Handwriting Practice Made Fun: Jokes, Riddles, Stories, and More!

- ☐ My child needs both letter and sentence handwriting practice (Choose Book #4)
- ☐ My child needs just handwriting practice with sentences (Choose Book #5)

Riddle

Trace the question.

The more you take away from me, the larger I become. What am I?

Copy the question.

☐ Starts with capital letter ☐ Finger spaces between words ☐ Ends with a punctuation mark

Trace the answer.

a hole

Copy the answer.

Silly Story Word Choices

Trace the words in each list.

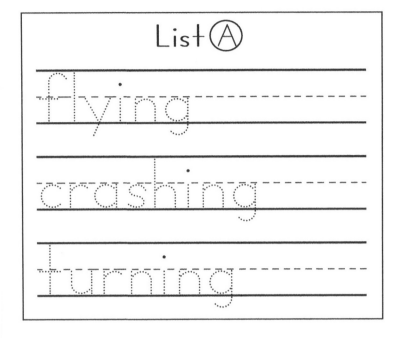
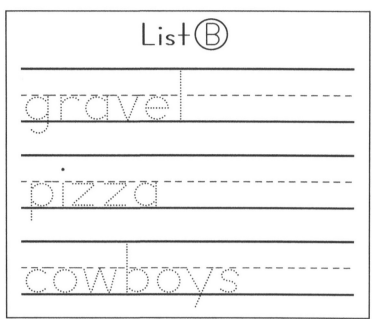
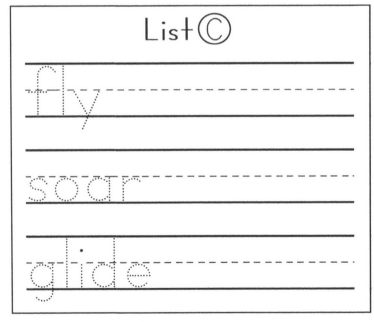
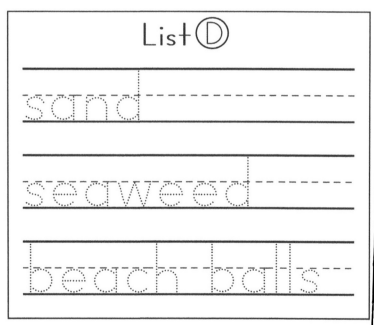

List A: flying, crashing, turning

List B: gravel, pizza, cowboys

List C: fly, soar, glide

List D: sand, seaweed, beach balls

Next, choose <u>one</u> word from each list and circle it. Then, copy the four words that you selected into the appropriate spots on the next page.

Silly Story

Write the words that you circled from the previous page in the correct spot for Lists A, B, C, and D. Then, read your silly story.

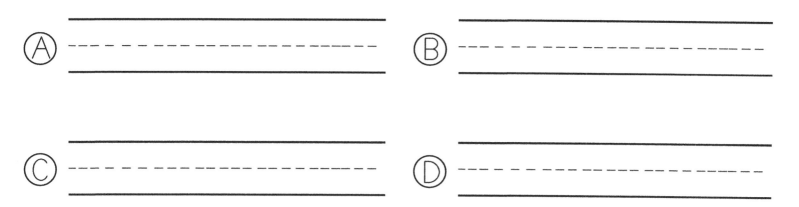

Seagulls haven't always lived by the sea. First, they lived by the bay and were called Bay-gulls. But, there wasn't enough cream cheese by the bay. Then, they lived in the forest and were called Tree-gulls. However, there wasn't much space to fly in the forest. They kept Ⓐ into trees. So, they moved to the mountains, where they were called Rock-gulls. However, there weren't any fish to eat in the mountains. There was only dust and Ⓑ. So, they moved to the sea. There was plenty of room to Ⓒ by the sea, and all the Ⓓ they could eat. So, that is where they decided to stay.

Fun Fact

Trace the fact.

It is impossible to lick your own elbow.

Copy the fact.

☐ Starts with capital letter ☐ Finger spaces between words ☐ Ends with a punctuation mark

Draw the fact.

Crack the Code

a	b	c	d	e	f	g	h	i	j	k	l	m
1	2	3	4	5	6	7	8	9	10	11	12	13

n	o	p	q	r	s	t	u	v	w	x	y	z
14	15	16	17	18	19	20	21	22	23	24	25	26

Decode the sentence.

1 14   1 22 5 18 1 7 5

25 1 23 14   12 1 19 20 19

19 9 24   19 5 3 15 14 4 19

☐ Starts with capital letter   ☐ Finger spaces between words   ☐ Ends with a punctuation mark

Joke

Trace the question.

What do you call a pig
that knows karate?

Copy the question.

☐ Starts with capital letter   ☐ Finger spaces between words   ☐ Ends with a punctuation mark

Trace the answer.

a pork chop

Copy the answer.

Riddle

Trace the question.

I go up and down, but I never move. What am I?

Copy the question.

☐ Starts with capital letter ☐ Finger spaces between words ☐ Ends with a punctuation mark

Trace the answer.

a staircase

Copy the answer.

Silly Story Word Choices

Trace the words in each list.

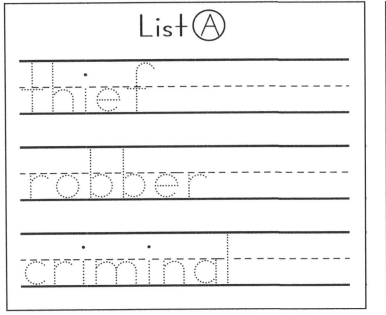

List Ⓐ
- thief
- robber
- criminal

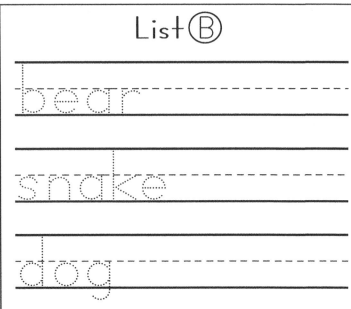

List Ⓑ
- bear
- snake
- dog

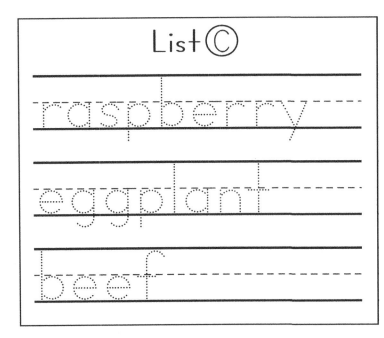

List Ⓒ
- raspberry
- eggplant
- beef

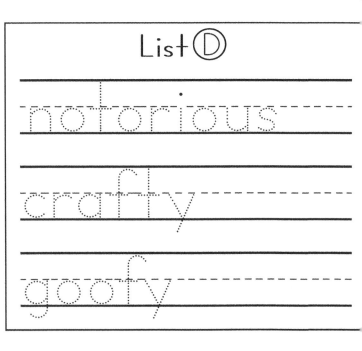

List Ⓓ
- notorious
- crafty
- goofy

Next, choose <u>one</u> word from each list and circle it. Then, copy the four words that you selected into the appropriate spots on the next page.

Silly Story

Write the words that you circled from the previous page in the correct spot for Lists A, B, C, and D. Then, read your silly story.

Ⓐ ------------------------------   Ⓑ ------------------------------

Ⓒ ------------------------------   Ⓓ ------------------------------

Detective May was struggling to solve her latest crime. Diane's Donut store had been robbed. The Ⓐ had stolen every donut they had, and there were no clues to be found anywhere. So, Detective May decided to use the police Ⓑ to sniff for clues. It sniffed all over town and eventually found some of Diane's special Ⓒ donut jelly on the doorstep of the Ⓓ candy thief, Sally Sugarpuff. When Detective May broke into her house, she found stolen donuts from floor to ceiling. Sally Sugarpuff was sentenced to ten years of eating nothing but carrots and rice.

Fun Fact

Trace the fact.

A crocodile cannot stick out its tongue.

Copy the fact.

☐ Starts with capital letter   ☐ Finger spaces between words   ☐ Ends with a punctuation mark

Draw the fact.

Crack the Code

a	b	c	d	e	f	g	h	i	j	k	l	m
1	2	3	4	5	6	7	8	9	10	11	12	13

n	o	p	q	r	s	t	u	v	w	x	y	z
14	15	16	17	18	19	20	21	22	23	24	25	26

Decode the sentence.

7 9 18 1 6 6 5 19

8 1 22 5   2 12 1 3 11

20 15 14 7 21 5 19

☐ Starts with capital letter   ☐ Finger spaces between words   ☐ Ends with a punctuation mark

Joke

Trace the question.

Why can't a cheetah play hide and seek?

Copy the question.

☐ Starts with capital letter ☐ Finger spaces between words ☐ Ends with a punctuation mark

Trace the answer.

because he's always spotted

Copy the answer.

Riddle

Trace the question.

I have many keys but I can't open a single lock. What am I?

Copy the question.

☐ Starts with capital letter ☐ Finger spaces between words ☐ Ends with a punctuation mark

Trace the answer.

a piano

Copy the answer.

Silly Story Word Choices

Trace the words in each list.

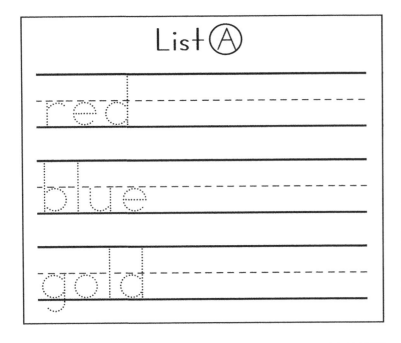

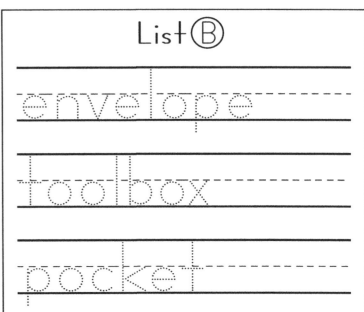

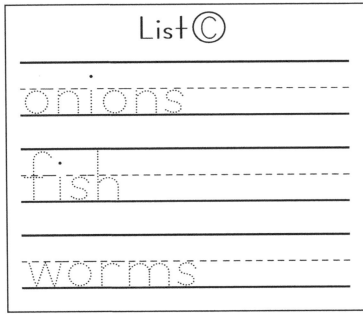

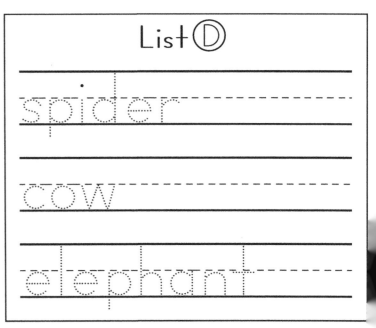

Next, choose <u>one</u> word from each list and circle it. Then, copy the four words that you selected into the appropriate spots on the next page.

Silly Story

Write the words that you circled from the previous page in the correct spot for Lists A, B, C, and D. Then, read your silly story.

Ⓐ ------------------------------

Ⓑ ------------------------------

Ⓒ ------------------------------

Ⓓ ------------------------------

There was once a little girl who loved to eat her lunch in the forest. One day, she went to the forest to eat. She sat in her usual spot, on the big Ⓐ toadstool. Then, she opened her Ⓑ and took out her sandwich. The sandwich had her favorite filling inside, cheese and Ⓒ. But just as she was about to take a bite, an enormous Ⓓ landed on her knee and frightened her away. When she nervously returned a few hours later, she saw that the Ⓓ had eaten everything. From that day onwards, she never ate her lunch on the toadstool again.

Fun Fact

Trace the fact.

An octopus has nine
brains.

Copy the fact.

☐ Starts with capital letter ☐ Finger spaces between words ☐ Ends with a punctuation mark

Draw the fact.

Crack the Code

a	b	c	d	e	f	g	h	i	j	k	l	m
1	2	3	4	5	6	7	8	9	10	11	12	13

n	o	p	q	r	s	t	u	v	w	x	y	z
14	15	16	17	18	19	20	21	22	23	24	25	26

Decode the sentence.

13 15 19 20   16 5 15 16 12 5

6 1 12 12   1 19 12 5 5 16

9 14   19 5 22 5 14

13 9 14 21 20 5 19

☐ Starts with capital letter   ☐ Finger spaces between words   ☐ Ends with a punctuation mark

Joke

Trace the question.

How does a cow do math?

Copy the question.

☐ Starts with capital letter   ☐ Finger spaces between words   ☐ Ends with a punctuation mark

Trace the answer.

with a cowculator

Copy the answer.

Riddle

Trace the question.

I have lots of eyes, but
I can't see. What am I?

Copy the question.

☐ Starts with capital letter   ☐ Finger spaces between words   ☐ Ends with a punctuation mark

Trace the answer.

a potato

Copy the answer.

Silly Story Word Choices

Trace the words in each list.

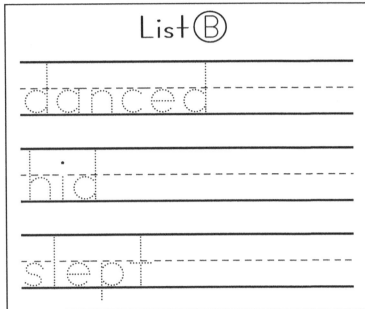
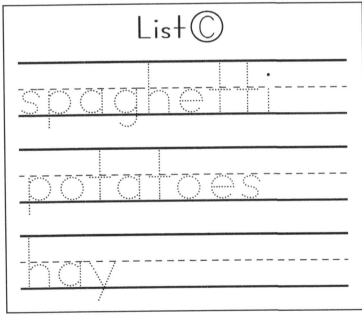
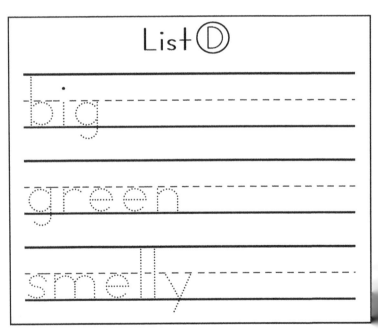

List A: cows, sheep, sausages
List B: danced, hid, slept
List C: spaghetti, potatoes, hay
List D: big, green, smelly

Next, choose <u>one</u> word from each list and circle it. Then, copy the four words that you selected into the appropriate spots on the next page.

Silly Story

Write the words that you circled from the previous page in the correct spot for Lists A, B, C, and D. Then, read your silly story.

Ⓐ _____   Ⓑ _____

Ⓒ _____   Ⓓ _____

There once was a little tractor called Trevor. He hated living on the farm because he was afraid of Ⓐ. Every time he saw one, he drove away and Ⓑ in the barn behind a pile of Ⓒ. Try as they did, his parents, Carrie the combine harvester and Tom the truck, couldn't find a way to make Trevor enjoy his life on the farm. So, when Trevor was old enough, he went to live in the Ⓓ city. Tractors weren't often seen in the Ⓓ city, so Trevor was a novelty. He was so novel that he became famous and went into showbusiness.

Fun Fact

Trace the fact.

It is impossible to sneeze
with your eyes open.

Copy the fact.

☐ Starts with capital letter   ☐ Finger spaces between words   ☐ Ends with a punctuation mark

Draw the fact.

Crack the Code

a	b	c	d	e	f	g	h	i	j	k	l	m
1	2	3	4	5	6	7	8	9	10	11	12	13

n	o	p	q	r	s	t	u	v	w	x	y	z
14	15	16	17	18	19	20	21	22	23	24	25	26

Decode the sentence.

13 15 19 20   9 14 19 5 20 19

8 1 20 3 8   6 18 15 13

5 7 7 19

☐ Starts with capital letter   ☐ Finger spaces between words   ☐ Ends with a punctuation mark

Joke

Trace the question.

What did one wall say to
the other wall?

Copy the question.

☐ Starts with capital letter   ☐ Finger spaces between words   ☐ Ends with a punctuation mark

Trace the answer.

I'll meet you at the
corner.

Copy the answer.

☐ Starts with capital letter   ☐ Finger spaces between words   ☐ Ends with a punctuation mark

Riddle

Trace the question.

I have only one eye, but
I can't see. What am I?

Copy the question.

☐ Starts with capital letter   ☐ Finger spaces between words   ☐ Ends with a punctuation mark

Trace the answer.

a needle

Copy the answer.

Silly Story Word Choices

Trace the words in each list.

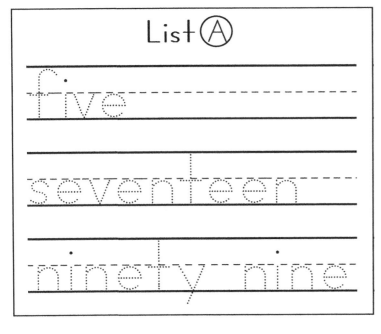

List Ⓐ
- five
- seventeen
- ninety-nine

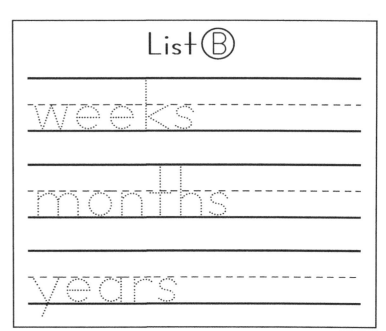

List Ⓑ
- weeks
- months
- years

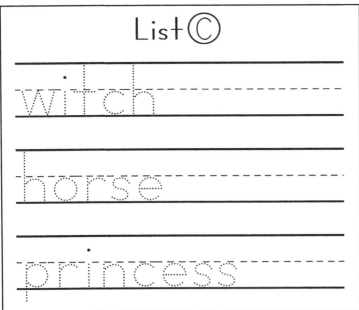

List Ⓒ
- witch
- horse
- princess

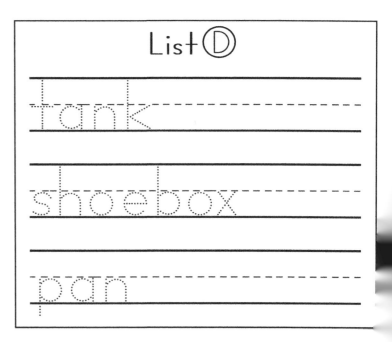

List Ⓓ
- tank
- shoebox
- pan

Next, choose <u>one</u> word from each list and circle it. Then, copy the four words that you selected into the appropriate spots on the next page.

Silly Story

Write the words that you circled from the previous page in the correct spot for Lists A, B, C, and D. Then, read your silly story.

Ⓐ _____   Ⓑ _____

Ⓒ _____   Ⓓ _____

Mrs. Finch ran a pet shop. One day she got a delivery of new pets that included Ⓐ cats, three dogs, fourteen goldfish, and one small dragon. It was easy to sell the cats, dogs, and fish. But selling the dragon was much harder. She couldn't sell it for Ⓑ ! Nobody seemed to want a dragon. Luckily, after a while, a Ⓒ came to the shop. "A dragon?" she said, "I've been looking for a dragon for years. I'll take it!" And so, she left with the dragon and a great big Ⓓ to keep it in.

Fun Fact

Trace the fact.

Slugs have four noses.

Copy the fact.

☐ Starts with capital letter   ☐ Finger spaces between words   ☐ Ends with a punctuation mark

Draw the fact.

Crack the Code

Decode the sentence.

A group of

hippos is

called a

bloat.

☐ Starts with capital letter   ☐ Finger spaces between words   ☐ Ends with a punctuation mark

Joke

Trace the question.

Why did they stop giving tests at the zoo?

Copy the question.

☐ Starts with capital letter   ☐ Finger spaces between words   ☐ Ends with a punctuation mark

Trace the answer.

because it was full of cheetahs

Copy the answer.

Riddle

Trace the question.

I have two hands, but I cannot clap. What am I?

Copy the question.

☐ Starts with capital letter   ☐ Finger spaces between words   ☐ Ends with a punctuation mark

Trace the answer.

a clock

Copy the answer.

Silly Story Word Choices

Trace the words in each list.

List Ⓐ
- bored
- scared
- hungry

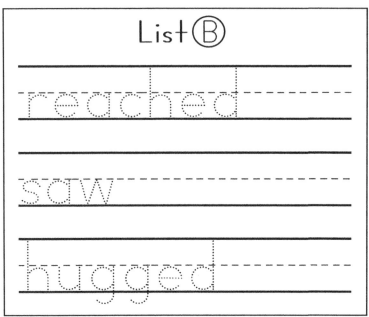

List Ⓑ
- reached
- saw
- hugged

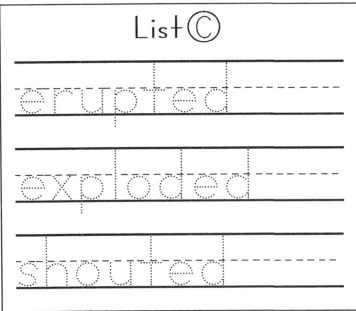

List Ⓒ
- erupted
- exploded
- shouted

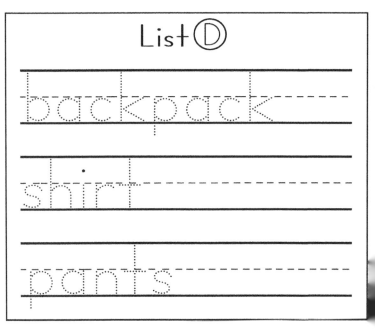

List Ⓓ
- backpack
- shirt
- pants

Next, choose <u>one</u> word from each list and circle it. Then, copy the four words that you selected into the appropriate spots on the next page.

Silly Story

Write the words that you circled from the previous page in the correct spot for Lists A, B, C, and D. Then, read your silly story.

Ⓐ _____   Ⓑ _____

Ⓒ _____   Ⓓ _____

There once was a man who lived at the foot of a mountain. One morning he was Ⓐ, so he decided to climb it. The mountain was very steep and taller than the clouds, so he knew the climb would be long. Indeed, the climb took him many months, and when he finally Ⓑ the top, he was very tired. "I'm so tired, I don't know if I have the energy to climb back down again," he said. But, little did he know, the mountain was actually a volcano. It Ⓒ, and the man rode back down on a river of lava, using his Ⓓ as a surfboard.

Fun Fact

Trace the fact.

Caterpillars have 12 eyes.

Copy the fact.

☐ Starts with capital letter   ☐ Finger spaces between words   ☐ Ends with a punctuation mark

Draw the fact.

Crack the Code

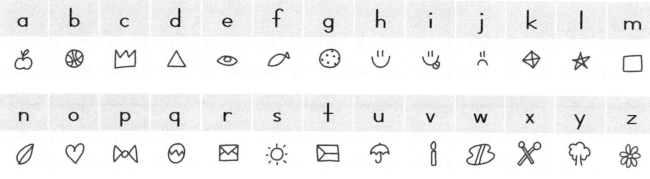

Decode the sentence.

Some fish

cough to

clear out

their gills.

☐ Starts with capital letter   ☐ Finger spaces between words   ☐ Ends with a punctuation mark

Joke

Trace the question.

Why are ghosts bad liars?

Copy the question.

☐ Starts with capital letter   ☐ Finger spaces between words   ☐ Ends with a punctuation mark

Trace the answer.

because you can see right through them.

Copy the answer.

Riddle

Trace the question.

I have four legs, but I cannot walk. What am I?

Copy the question.

☐ Starts with capital letter   ☐ Finger spaces between words   ☐ Ends with a punctuation mark

Trace the answer.

a table

Copy the answer.

Silly Story Word Choices

Trace the words in each list.

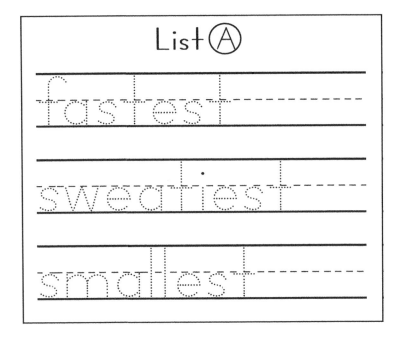

List A
- fastest
- sweatiest
- smallest

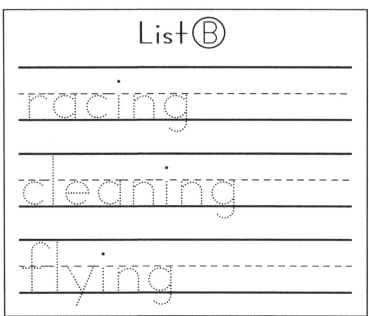

List B
- racing
- cleaning
- flying

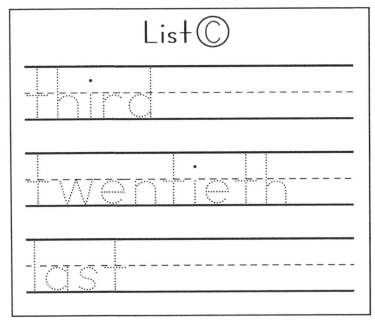

List C
- third
- twentieth
- last

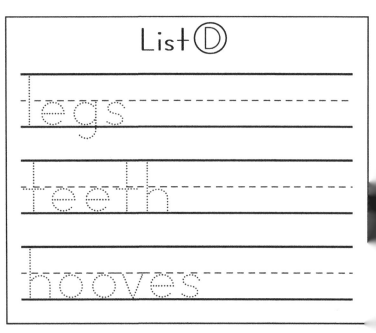

List D
- legs
- teeth
- hooves

Next, choose <u>one</u> word from each list and circle it. Then, copy the four words that you selected into the appropriate spots on the next page.

Silly Story

Write the words that you circled from the previous page in the correct spot for Lists A, B, C, and D. Then, read your silly story.

Ⓐ _____ Ⓑ _____

Ⓒ _____ Ⓓ _____

Jill was a jockey. She rode the Ⓐ horse in the world. A horse called Black Thunder. She had come first in the national horse race for seven years in a row. However, this year a new rule had been made. The rule stated that horses could be fitted with machinery if they wanted. Jill was great at Ⓑ, but not very good at mechanics. So, this year she lost. She came in Ⓒ place. In first place was a horse called Zippy. Zippy had bionic Ⓓ. In second place was a horse called Universe, Universe had rocket boosters.

Fun Fact

Trace the fact.

An ostrich's eye is bigger than its brain.

Copy the fact.

☐ Starts with capital letter   ☐ Finger spaces between words   ☐ Ends with a punctuation mark

Draw the fact.

Crack the Code

Decode the sentence.

_____

- - - - - - - - - - - - - - - - - - -

_____

🐟 ✉️ ♥️ 🍪 ☀️   △ ✉️ ✌️ 🍃 ◇

_____

- - - - - - - - - - - - - - - - - - -

_____

🎨 🍎 ✉️ 👁 ✉️

_____

- - - - - - - - - - - - - - - - - - -

_____

✉️ ☺️ ✉️ ♥️ ☂️ 🍪 ☺️

_____

- - - - - - - - - - - - - - - - - - -

_____

✉️ ☺️ 👁 ✌️ ✉️   ☀️ ◇ ✌️ 🍃

☐ Starts with capital letter   ☐ Finger spaces between words   ☐ Ends with a punctuation mark

Joke

Trace the question.

Why do shoemakers go to heaven?

Copy the question.

☐ Starts with capital letter   ☐ Finger spaces between words   ☐ Ends with a punctuation mark

Trace the answer.

because they have good soles

Copy the answer.

Riddle

Trace the question.

I have many teeth, but I can't bite. What am I?

Copy the question.

☐ Starts with capital letter   ☐ Finger spaces between words   ☐ Ends with a punctuation mark

Trace the answer.

a comb

Copy the answer.

Silly Story Word Choices

Trace the words in each list.

List Ⓐ
shoe
sock
jar

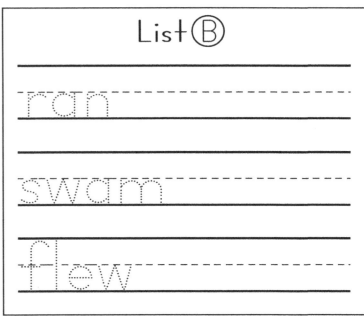

List Ⓑ
ran
swam
flew

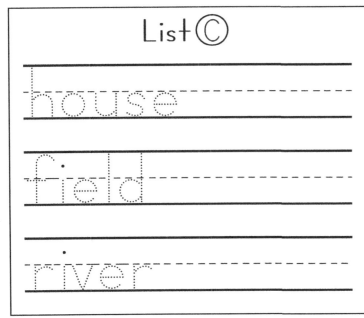

List Ⓒ
house
field
river

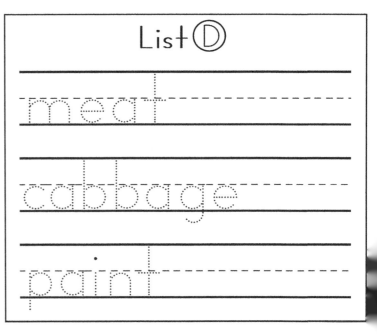

List Ⓓ
meat
cabbage
paint

Next, choose <u>one</u> word from each list and circle it. Then, copy the four words that you selected into the appropriate spots on the next page.

Silly Story

Write the words that you circled from the previous page in the correct spot for Lists A, B, C, and D. Then, read your silly story.

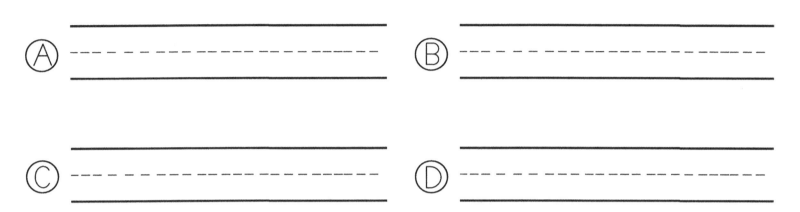

There once was a mouse that lived in a Ⓐ. He had four mouse sisters, a mouse mom, and a mouse dad. One day, his mouse dad was injured by a cat and couldn't go out to find cheese for them to eat, as he usually did. His mouse mom had to look after his sisters, so it was up to him to feed the family. The mouse Ⓑ out and searched the whole Ⓒ. He couldn't find cheese anywhere, so he returned with some Ⓓ instead. Luckily, his family liked this very much. They all went to bed with full stomachs.

Fun Fact

Trace the fact.

Kangaroos and emus can't walk backwards.

Copy the fact.

☐ Starts with capital letter   ☐ Finger spaces between words   ☐ Ends with a punctuation mark

Draw the fact.

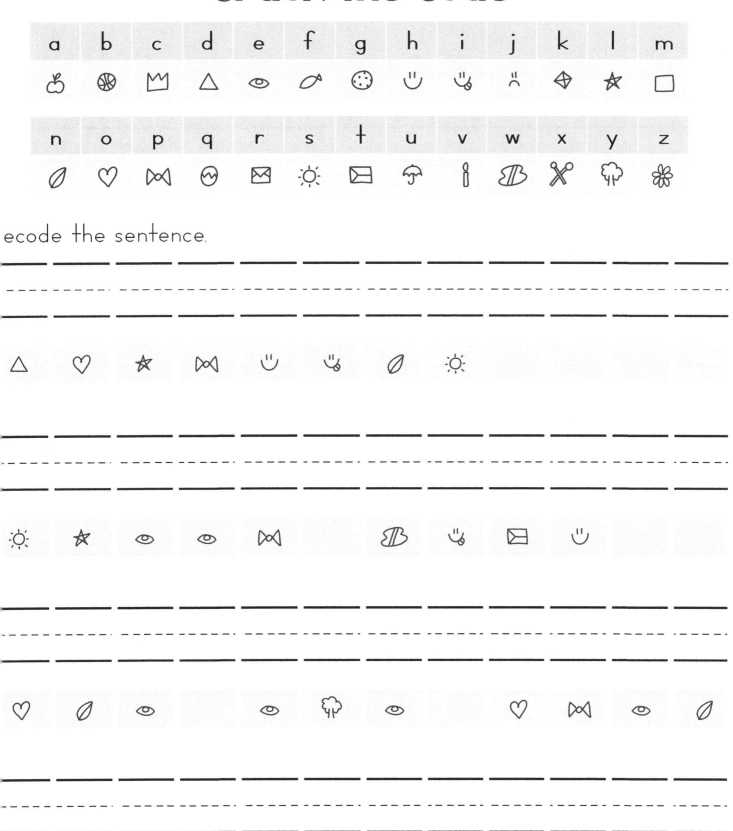

Joke

Trace the question.

What nails do carpenters hate hammering?

Copy the question.

☐ Starts with capital letter ☐ Finger spaces between words ☐ Ends with a punctuation mark

Trace the answer.

fingernails

Copy the answer.

Riddle

Trace the question.

I have lots of words, but I never speak. What am I?

Copy the question.

☐ Starts with capital letter ☐ Finger spaces between words ☐ Ends with a punctuation mark

Trace the answer.

a book

Copy the answer.

Silly Story Word Choices

Trace the words in each list.

List Ⓐ
- crumb
- tooth
- pea

List Ⓑ
- lift
- swing
- sharpen

List Ⓒ
- high
- quiet
- annoying

List Ⓓ
- wiggle
- hop
- dance

Next, choose <u>one</u> word from each list and circle it. Then, copy the four words that you selected into the appropriate spots on the next page.

Silly Story

Write the words that you circled from the previous page in the correct spot for Lists A, B, C, and D. Then, read your silly story.

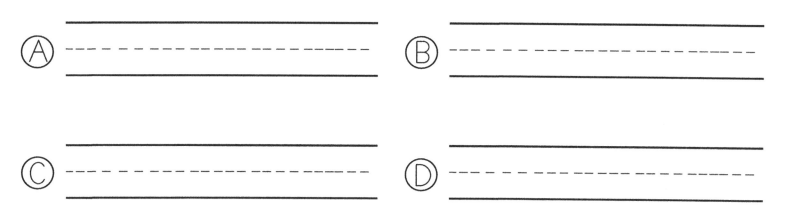

There once was a very, very small woman. She was no bigger than a Ⓐ. She had tried so many different jobs, but she was no good at any of them. She tried being a chef, but she wasn't strong enough to Ⓑ a knife. She tried being a taxi driver, but she was too small to see over the steering wheel. She even tried to be a singer, but her voice was so Ⓒ that nobody could hear it. However, one day, she got a job as a computer fixer. She could Ⓓ in between the keys and fix the computers from the inside. This job was perfect for her.

Fun Fact

Trace the fact.

A group of frogs is called an army.

Copy the fact.

☐ Starts with capital letter   ☐ Finger spaces between words   ☐ Ends with a punctuation mark

Draw the fact.

Joke

Trace the question.

How do you stop a bull
from charging?

Copy the question.

☐ Starts with capital letter   ☐ Finger spaces between words   ☐ Ends with a punctuation mark

Trace the answer.

Take away its credit card

Copy the answer.

Riddle

Trace the question.

I have a head and a tail,
but no body. What am
I?

Copy the question.

☐ Starts with capital letter   ☐ Finger spaces between words   ☐ Ends with a punctuation mark

Trace the answer.

a coin

Copy the answer.

Silly Story Word Choices

Trace the words in each list.

List A
- California
- Jamaica
- Alaska

List B
- searched
- sniffed
- scuttled

List C
- boy
- fish
- elf

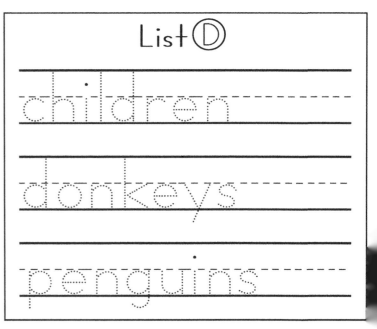

List D
- children
- donkeys
- penguins

Next, choose <u>one</u> word from each list and circle it. Then, copy the four words that you selected into the appropriate spots on the next page.

Silly Story

Write the words that you circled from the previous page in the correct spot for Lists A, B, C, and D. Then, read your silly story.

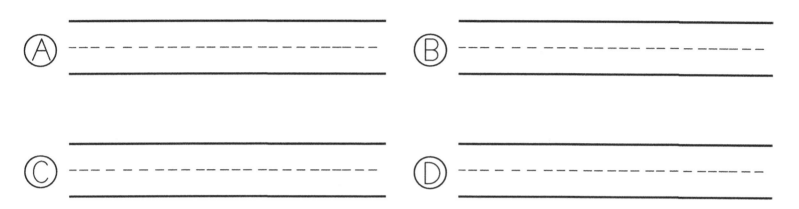

Ⓐ _____ Ⓑ _____

Ⓒ _____ Ⓓ _____

Caroline was a crab who lived on the coast of Ⓐ. One day she decided to move out from under her parent's rock to find a home of her own. She Ⓑ all day, but found nothing. But, on her way home, she discovered a castle made of sand. The castle had been built by a little Ⓒ earlier that day. She moved in and was happy. But the ocean washed it away in the middle of the night, and when she woke the next morning, she had to start her search all over again. Luckily, Ⓓ built new sandcastles every day.

Fun Fact

Trace the fact.

Hummingbirds can fly
backwards.

Copy the fact.

☐ Starts with capital letter ☐ Finger spaces between words ☐ Ends with a punctuation mark

Draw the fact.

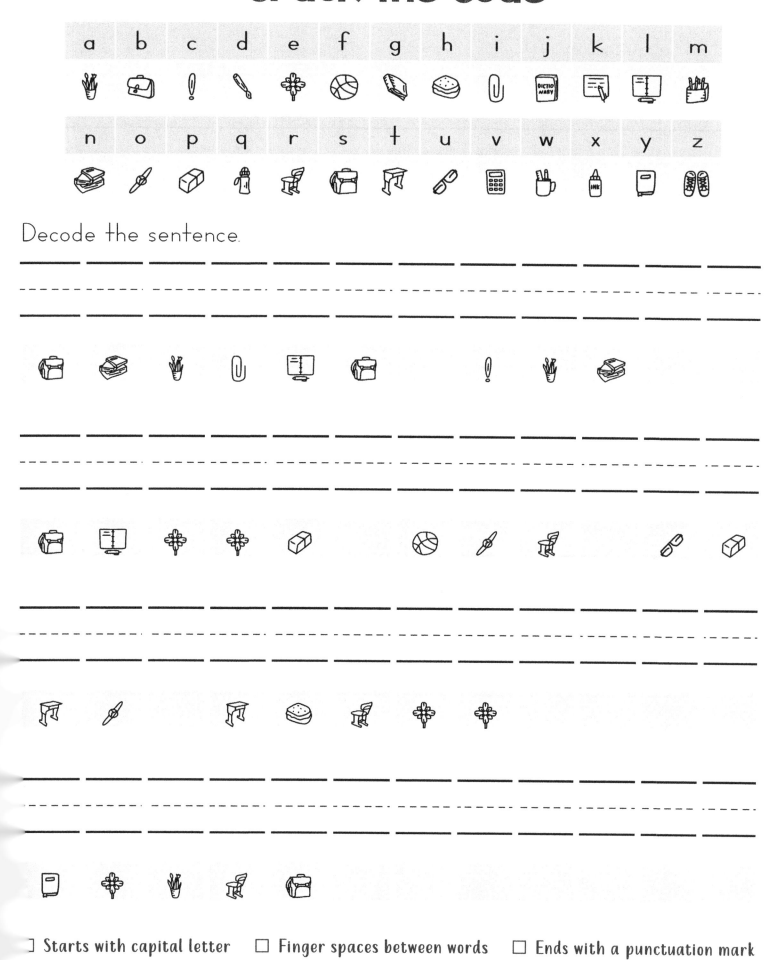

Joke

Trace the question.

Why do the French eat snails?

Copy the question.

☐ Starts with capital letter   ☐ Finger spaces between words   ☐ Ends with a punctuation mark

Trace the answer.

because they don't like fast food

Copy the answer.

Riddle

Trace the question.

I run all around a backyard, but I never move. What am I?

Copy the question.

☐ Starts with capital letter   ☐ Finger spaces between words   ☐ Ends with a punctuation mark

Trace the answer.

a fence

Copy the answer.

Silly Story Word Choices

Trace the words in each list.

List A
- strong
- funny
- cool

List B
- design
- write
- prepare

List C
- burped
- screamed
- sang

List D
- frog
- house
- banana

Next, choose <u>one</u> word from each list and circle it. Then, copy the four words that you selected into the appropriate spots on the next page.

Silly Story

Write the words that you circled from the previous page in the correct spot for Lists A, B, C, and D. Then, read your silly story.

Ⓐ _____ Ⓑ _____

Ⓒ _____ Ⓓ _____

There once was a wizard called Dribble. Dribble wasn't as Ⓐ as the other wizards, so they used to make fun of him. One day he'd had enough of being bullied, and decided to Ⓑ a magic spell that would show them he should be taken seriously. Once he had written the spell, he decided to try it out on one of the bullies. He didn't know exactly what it would do. He pointed his wand at Mabel the Meany, and Ⓒ "Zoom-Zoom Macaroon!". There was a loud 'pop', and Mabel turned into an Ⓓ.

Fun Fact

Trace the fact.

Dolphins shut off half their brain when sleeping.

Copy the fact.

☐ Starts with capital letter   ☐ Finger spaces between words   ☐ Ends with a punctuation mark

Draw the fact.

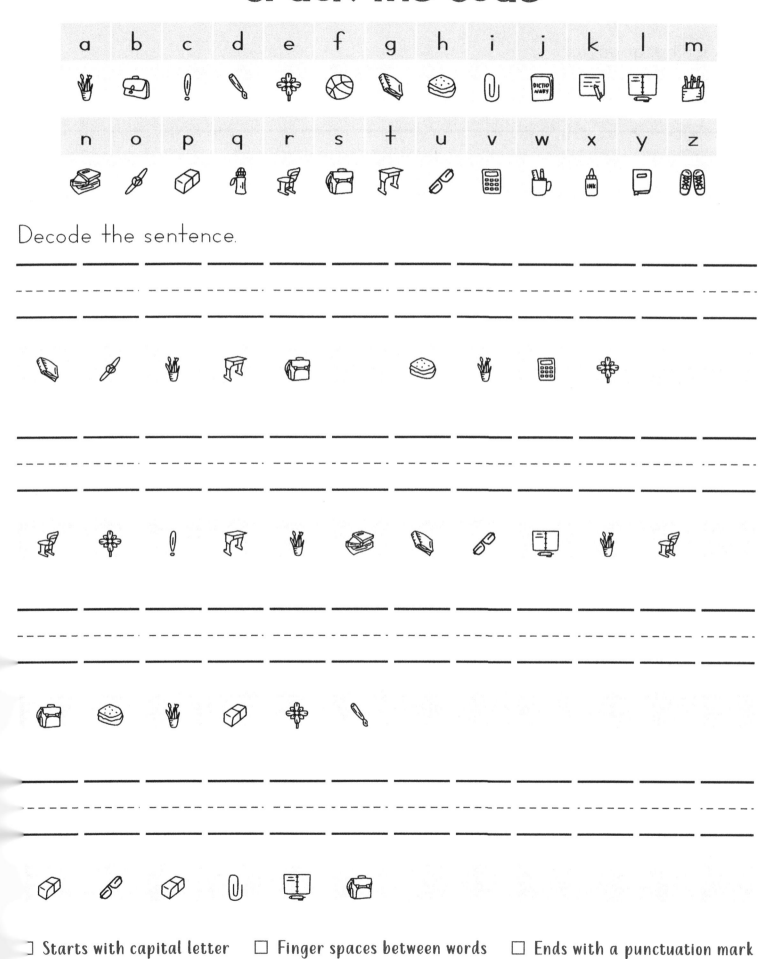

Joke

Trace the question.

Why didn't the sun go to college?

Copy the question.

☐ Starts with capital letter   ☐ Finger spaces between words   ☐ Ends with a punctuation mark

Trace the answer.

because it already had a million degrees

Copy the answer.

Riddle

Trace the question.

I am full of holes, but I can still hold water. What am I?

Copy the question.

☐ Starts with capital letter   ☐ Finger spaces between words   ☐ Ends with a punctuation mark

Trace the answer.

a sponge

Copy the answer.

Silly Story Word Choices

Trace the words in each list.

List Ⓐ
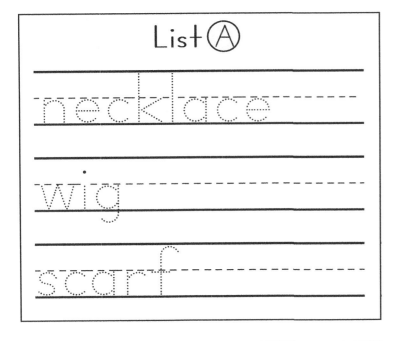
necklace
wig
scarf

List Ⓑ

private
silly
secret

List Ⓒ
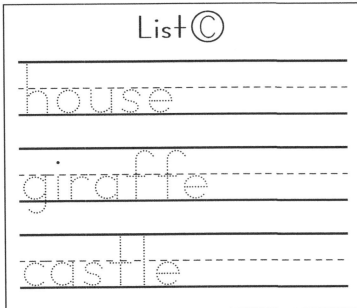
house
giraffe
castle

List Ⓓ
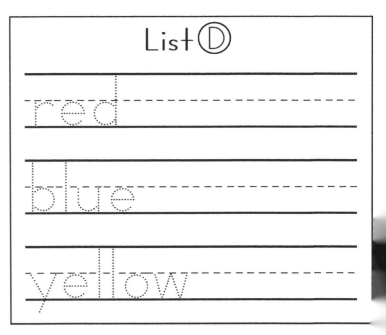
red
blue
yellow

Next, choose <u>one</u> word from each list and circle it. Then, copy the four words that you selected into the appropriate spots on the next page.

Silly Story

Write the words that you circled from the previous page in the correct spot for Lists A, B, C, and D. Then, read your silly story.

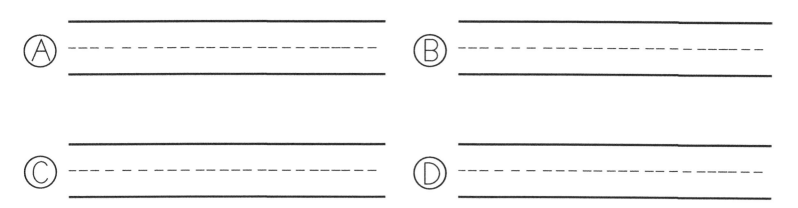

Ⓐ _____ Ⓑ _____

Ⓒ _____ Ⓓ _____

There was once a woman who had a magic Ⓐ . When she put it on, she turned invisible. She used it in all kinds of naughty ways. She would listen to people's Ⓑ conversations. She would sneak onto airplanes without paying or showing her passport. She would even steal candy from the store. But, one day she got caught. She was trying to scare a man who was painting the outside of a Ⓒ. She wobbled his ladder. He was so afraid that he kicked his paint off the ladder. The paint spilled all over the woman. Not only was she now bright Ⓓ all over, but she had been caught!

Fun Fact

Trace the fact.

Gorillas burp when they are happy.

Copy the fact.

☐ Starts with capital letter ☐ Finger spaces between words ☐ Ends with a punctuation mark

Draw the fact.

Joke

Trace the question.

What did you learn in school today?

Copy the question.

☐ Starts with capital letter   ☐ Finger spaces between words   ☐ Ends with a punctuation mark

Trace the answer.

Not enough! I need to go back tomorrow.

Copy the answer.

☐ Starts with capital letter   ☐ Finger spaces between words   ☐ Ends with a punctuation mar

Riddle

Trace the question.

I can't talk, but I will
reply when spoken to.
What am I?

Copy the question.

☐ Starts with capital letter   ☐ Finger spaces between words   ☐ Ends with a punctuation mark

Trace the answer.

an echo

Copy the answer.

Silly Story Word Choices

Trace the words in each list.

List Ⓐ
- cake
- gingerbread
- crackers

List Ⓑ
- crumbled
- shrunk
- screamed

List Ⓒ
- walls
- floors
- doors

List Ⓓ
- old
- strong
- dusty

Next, choose <u>one</u> word from each list and circle it. Then, copy the four words that you selected into the appropriate spots on the next page.

Silly Story

Write the words that you circled from the previous page in the correct spot for Lists A, B, C, and D. Then, read your silly story.

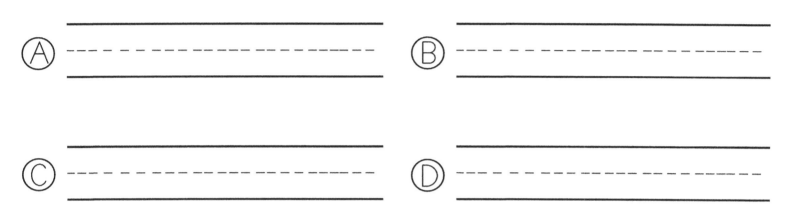

During the great brick shortage of 1992, many builders struggled to find another thing to make houses out of. Lisa the builder tried making houses out of Ⓐ , but they Ⓑ whenever it rained. Nick the contractor tried making houses out of cardboard, but mail carriers kept stealing the Ⓒ to make packaging. However, Glen the bricklayer had a bright idea. He started making houses out of big boring books. They were very Ⓓ, the same shape as bricks, and nobody wanted to read them anyway! They worked perfectly.

Fun Fact

Trace the fact.

Elephants can detect sound with their feet.

Copy the fact.

☐ Starts with capital letter   ☐ Finger spaces between words   ☐ Ends with a punctuation mark

Draw the fact.

Crack the Code

Decode the sentence.

☐ Starts with capital letter   ☐ Finger spaces between words   ☐ Ends with a punctuation mark

Joke

Trace the question.

What do bunnies like to
do at the store?

Copy the question.

☐ Starts with capital letter   ☐ Finger spaces between words   ☐ Ends with a punctuation mark

Trace the answer.

shop 'til they hop

Copy the answer.

Riddle

Trace the question.

I have many needles, but I don't sew. What am I?

Copy the question.

☐ Starts with capital letter ☐ Finger spaces between words ☐ Ends with a punctuation mark

Trace the answer.

a pine tree

Copy the answer.

Silly Story Word Choices

Trace the words in each list.

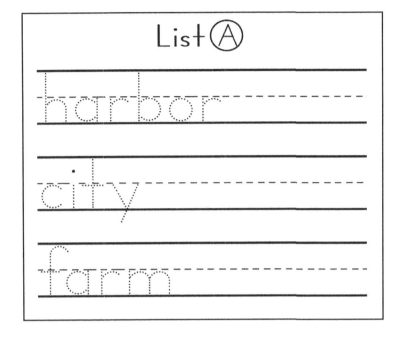

List A
- harbor
- city
- farm

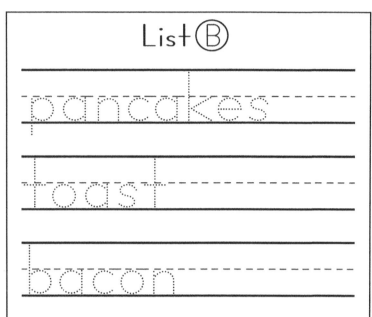

List B
- pancakes
- toast
- bacon

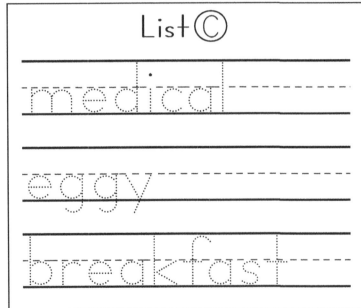

List C
- medical
- eggy
- breakfast

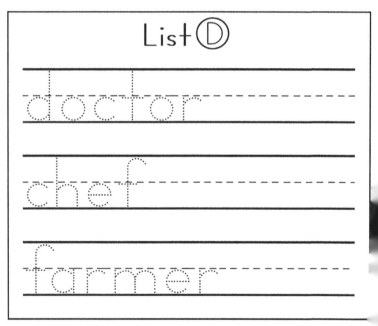

List D
- doctor
- chef
- farmer

Next, choose <u>one</u> word from each list and circle it. Then, copy the four words that you selected into the appropriate spots on the next page.

Silly Story

Write the words that you circled from the previous page in the correct spot for Lists A, B, C, and D. Then, read your silly story.

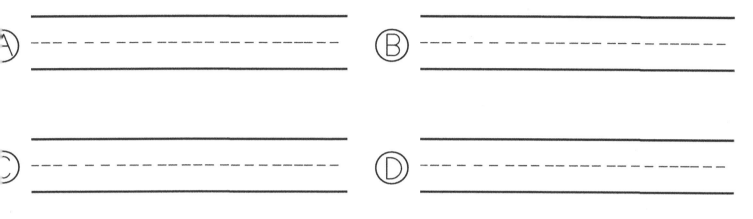

Once upon a time, an egg named Humpty decided he wanted to see the view of the Ⓐ . To see the view, he had to climb on top of a very tall wall. But, when he tried to sit down on the wall, he struggled to balance. He fell off. He zoomed downwards and smashed all over the ground, which was made of Ⓑ . The king's men arrived on horses and tried to put him back together. Unfortunately, king's men are not very good at dealing with Ⓒ emergencies. Neither are horses. Perhaps they should have called a Ⓓ instead.

Fun Fact

Trace the fact.

Horses and cows can sleep standing up.

Copy the fact.

☐ Starts with capital letter   ☐ Finger spaces between words   ☐ Ends with a punctuation mark

Draw the fact.

Joke

Trace the question.

What is corn's favorite
type of music?

Copy the question.

what is corns favorite hype of ~~music~~

music?

☐ Starts with capital letter ☐ Finger spaces between words ☐ Ends with a punctuation mark

Trace the answer.

pop

Copy the answer.

pop

Riddle

Trace the question.

I am at the end of everything. What am I?

Copy the question.

I am at the end of everything. what am I?

☑ Starts with capital letter ☐ Finger spaces between words ☐ Ends with a punctuation mark

Trace the answer.

the letter g

Copy the answer.

the letter g

Silly Story Word Choices

Trace the words in each list.

List A
- girl
- racoon
- bunny

List B
- disturb
- poke
- tickle

List C
- snacks
- socks
- bananas

List D
- sack
- crate
- ship

Next, choose <u>one</u> word from each list and circle it. Then, copy the four words that you selected into the appropriate spots on the next page.

Silly Story

Write the words that you circled from the previous page in the correct spot for Lists A, B, C, and D. Then, read your silly story.

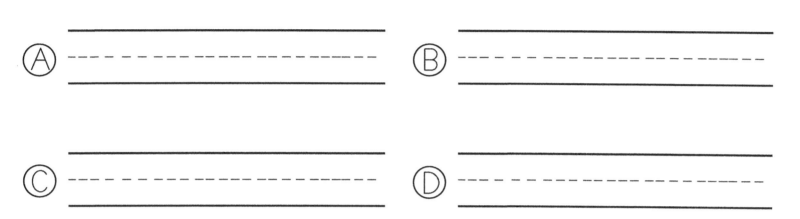

A Ⓐ named Jenny built a secret hideout in the woods. It was hidden in a cave, under the roots of a big tree. She loved her hideout because it was the only place nobody could Ⓑ her. But one day, she arrived at the hideout to find that a squirrel named Sammy was stealing her Ⓒ. She was angry at first and scared Sammy away. However, Sammy returned a little later with a Ⓓ full of fruit and nuts to apologize for what he had done. After that, Jenny and Sammy were best friends. They shared the hideout, and their Ⓒ.

Fun Fact

Trace the fact.

Your nose gets warmer when you lie.

Copy the fact.

☐ Starts with capital letter ☐ Finger spaces between words ☐ Ends with a punctuation mark

Draw the fact.

Joke

Trace the question.

Why did the frog take the bus to work?

Copy the question.

☐ Starts with capital letter ☐ Finger spaces between words ☐ Ends with a punctuation mark

Trace the answer.

because his car got toad

Copy the answer.

Riddle

Trace the question.

I come down, but I never go up. What am I?

Copy the question.

☐ Starts with capital letter   ☐ Finger spaces between words   ☐ Ends with a punctuation mark

Trace the answer.

rain

Copy the answer.

Silly Story Word Choices

Trace the words in each list.

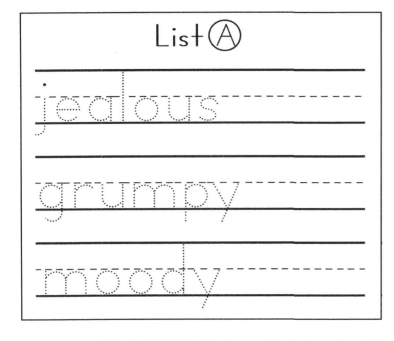

List Ⓐ

jealous

grumpy

moody

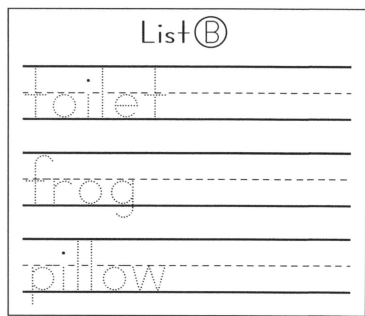

List Ⓑ

toilet

frog

pillow

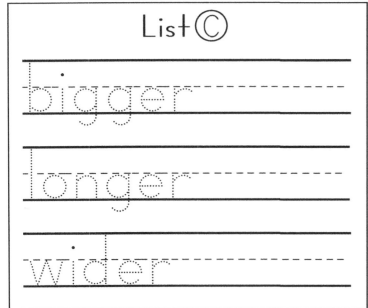

List Ⓒ

bigger

longer

wider

List Ⓓ

vegetable

flower

lollipop

Next, choose <u>one</u> word from each list and circle it. Then, copy the four words that you selected into the appropriate spots on the next page.

Silly Story

Write the words that you circled from the previous page in the correct spot for Lists A, B, C, and D. Then, read your silly story.

Ⓐ _____   Ⓑ _____

Ⓒ _____   Ⓓ _____

Gerald was a very Ⓐ gnome. He was always complaining that other gnomes had better stuff than him. Matilda had a wheelbarrow, Norris had a fishing pole, and Lorraine had a lovely blue Ⓑ to sit on. Gerald had nothing but a nose that was Ⓒ than everyone else's. But one day he smelled smoke! He realized the Ⓓ garden was on fire! He managed to warn his owner just in time to put the fire out and save the garden. It turns out he had a superpower. Super-Smell! A superpower, he thought, was much better than a wheelbarrow or a fishing pole.

Fun Fact

Trace the fact.

Lightning is five times hotter than the sun.

Copy the fact.

☐ Starts with capital letter ☐ Finger spaces between words ☐ Ends with a punctuation mark

Draw the fact.

Joke

Trace the question.

Why can't your hand be 12 inches long?

Copy the question.

☐ Starts with capital letter ☐ Finger spaces between words ☐ Ends with a punctuation mark

Trace the answer.

because then it would be a foot

Copy the answer.

Riddle

Trace the question.

I go up, but I never come down. What am I?

Copy the question.

☐ Starts with capital letter ☐ Finger spaces between words ☐ Ends with a punctuation mark

Trace the answer.

age

Copy the answer.

Silly Story Word Choices

Trace the words in each list.

List Ⓐ
- ate
- cooked
- read

List Ⓑ
- famous
- fabulous
- angry

List Ⓒ
- mouse
- cat
- lizard

List Ⓓ
- ears
- hair
- eyebrows

Next, choose <u>one</u> word from each list and circle it. Then, copy the four words that you selected into the appropriate spots on the next page.

Silly Story

Write the words that you circled from the previous page in the correct spot for Lists A, B, C, and D. Then, read your silly story.

Ⓐ _____   Ⓑ _____

Ⓒ _____   Ⓓ _____

There once was a chef who didn't know how to cook. He had been given the job by accident. He tried all sorts of things to learn to cook as quickly as possible. First, he Ⓐ ten cookbooks, but he still couldn't cook. Then he tried dressing up as the Ⓑ chef Jimmy Oscar, but he still couldn't cook. In the end, he hid a Ⓒ under his hat, who controlled him like a puppet by pulling his Ⓓ. The Ⓒ was a very talented chef, so this arrangement worked very well.

Fun Fact

Trace the fact.

Your heart beats about 100,000 times a day.

Copy the fact.

☐ Starts with capital letter   ☐ Finger spaces between words   ☐ Ends with a punctuation mark

Draw the fact.

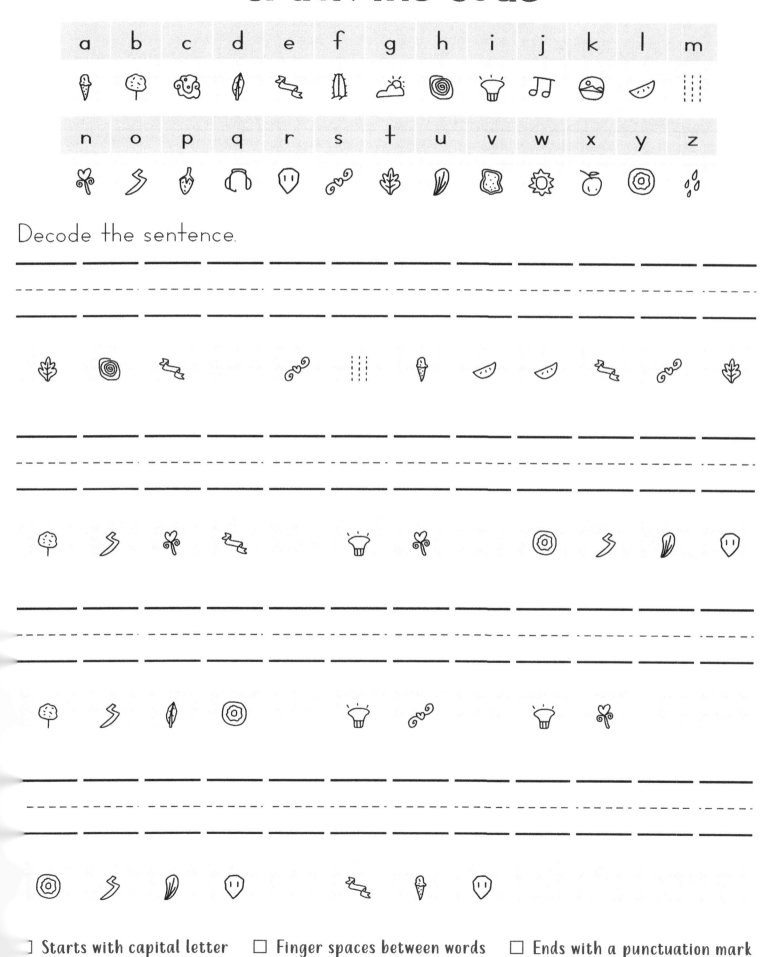

Joke

Trace the question.

How does a scientist
freshen their breath?

Copy the question.

☐ Starts with capital letter   ☐ Finger spaces between words   ☐ Ends with a punctuation mark

Trace the answer.

with experi mints

Copy the answer.

Riddle

Trace the question.

I have a neck, but no head. What am I?

Copy the question.

☐ Starts with capital letter ☐ Finger spaces between words ☐ Ends with a punctuation mark

Trace the answer.

a bottle

Copy the answer.

Silly Story Word Choices

Trace the words in each list.

List Ⓐ
- floppy
- furry
- green

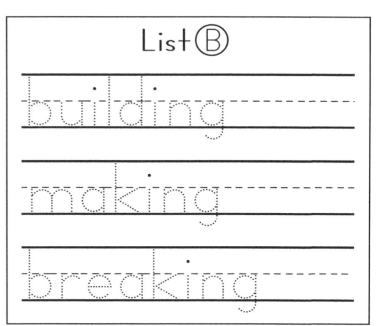

List Ⓑ
- building
- making
- breaking

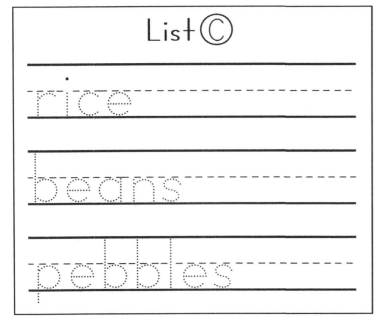

List Ⓒ
- rice
- beans
- pebbles

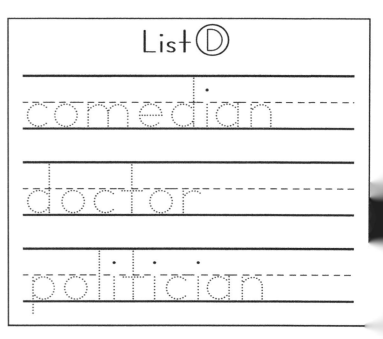

List Ⓓ
- comedian
- doctor
- politician

Next, choose <u>one</u> word from each list and circle it. Then, copy the four words that you selected into the appropriate spots on the next page.

Silly Story

Write the words that you circled from the previous page in the correct spot for Lists A, B, C, and D. Then, read your silly story.

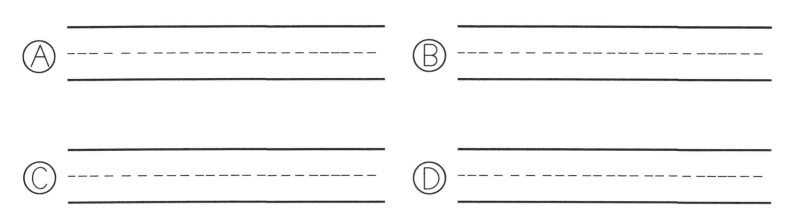

Pippa was a puppet who just wanted to live like a real-life girl. Nobody would take her seriously because she had a Ⓐ head and strings attached to her arms and legs. So, she visited an inventor. The inventor was really good at Ⓑ machines. So, he filled her wooden body with Ⓒ, bolts, and wires. Soon, she could stand up without any strings at all. Everybody now thought she was a real girl. She was now taken so seriously that she managed to get her dream job as a Ⓓ.

Fun Fact

Trace the fact.

Your heart is about the
same size as your fist.

Copy the fact.

☐ Starts with capital letter   ☐ Finger spaces between words   ☐ Ends with a punctuation mark

Draw the fact.

Joke

Trace the question.

What time is it when the clock strikes 13?

Copy the question.

☐ Starts with capital letter   ☐ Finger spaces between words   ☐ Ends with a punctuation mark

Trace the answer.

time to get a new clock

Copy the answer.

Riddle

Trace the question.

I jump when I walk and sit when I stand. What am I?

Copy the question.

☐ Starts with capital letter ☐ Finger spaces between words ☐ Ends with a punctuation mark

Trace the answer.

a kangaroo

Copy the answer.

Silly Story Word Choices

Trace the words in each list.

List A
- sad
- annoyed
- upset

List B
- friendly
- jolly
- funny

List C
- chase
- catch
- scare

List D
- great
- silly
- amazing

Next, choose <u>one</u> word from each list and circle it. Then, copy the four words that you selected into the appropriate spots on the next page.

Silly Story

Write the words that you circled from the previous page in the correct spot for Lists A, B, C, and D. Then, read your silly story.

Ⓐ _____   Ⓑ _____

Ⓒ _____   Ⓓ _____

Julian the giant was Ⓐ. Everyone ran away from him because they thought he was mean, like other giants. But he wasn't mean at all. He was very Ⓑ. He was also very lonely and just wanted to make friends. But one day, he helped a girl escape from the mean giants. They were trying to Ⓒ her. She and Julian became Ⓓ friends. She introduced him to the people in her village, and they all saw that he was nothing to be afraid of. Julian moved into the village and had more friends than he knew what to do with!

Fun Fact

Trace the fact.

A shrimp's heart is located inside its head.

Copy the fact.

☐ Starts with capital letter ☐ Finger spaces between words ☐ Ends with a punctuation mark

Draw the fact.

Joke

Trace the question.

How does the moon cut its hair?

Copy the question.

☐ Starts with capital letter ☐ Finger spaces between words ☐ Ends with a punctuation mark

Trace the answer.

eclipse it

Copy the answer.

Riddle

Trace the question.

I am a nut with a hole.
What am I?

Copy the question.

☐ Starts with capital letter   ☐ Finger spaces between words   ☐ Ends with a punctuation mark

Trace the answer.

a doughnut

Copy the answer.

Silly Story Word Choices

Trace the words in each list.

List A
- parents
- rabbits
- dog

List B
- sneezed
- sawed
- danced

List C
- weeks
- months
- hours

List D
- bread
- cheese
- pancakes

Next, choose <u>one</u> word from each list and circle it. Then, copy the four words that you selected into the appropriate spots on the next page.

Silly Story

Write the words that you circled from the previous page in the correct spot for Lists A, B, C, and D. Then, read your silly story.

Ⓐ _____   Ⓑ _____

Ⓒ _____   Ⓓ _____

Bobby's friends all had bicycles. Bobby wished he had a bicycle as well, but his Ⓐ couldn't afford one. Luckily, Bobby was good at building things, so he decided to make one out of junk from the local junkyard. He hammered and Ⓑ for Ⓒ. In the end, he had the most unique bicycle anyone had ever seen. He made the wheels out of trash can lids, the handlebars out of spatulas, the seat out of a bowling ball, and the pedals out of Ⓓ.

Fun Fact

Trace the fact.

Hens lay around 230
eggs in a year.

Copy the fact.

☐ Starts with capital letter   ☐ Finger spaces between words   ☐ Ends with a punctuation mark

Draw the fact.

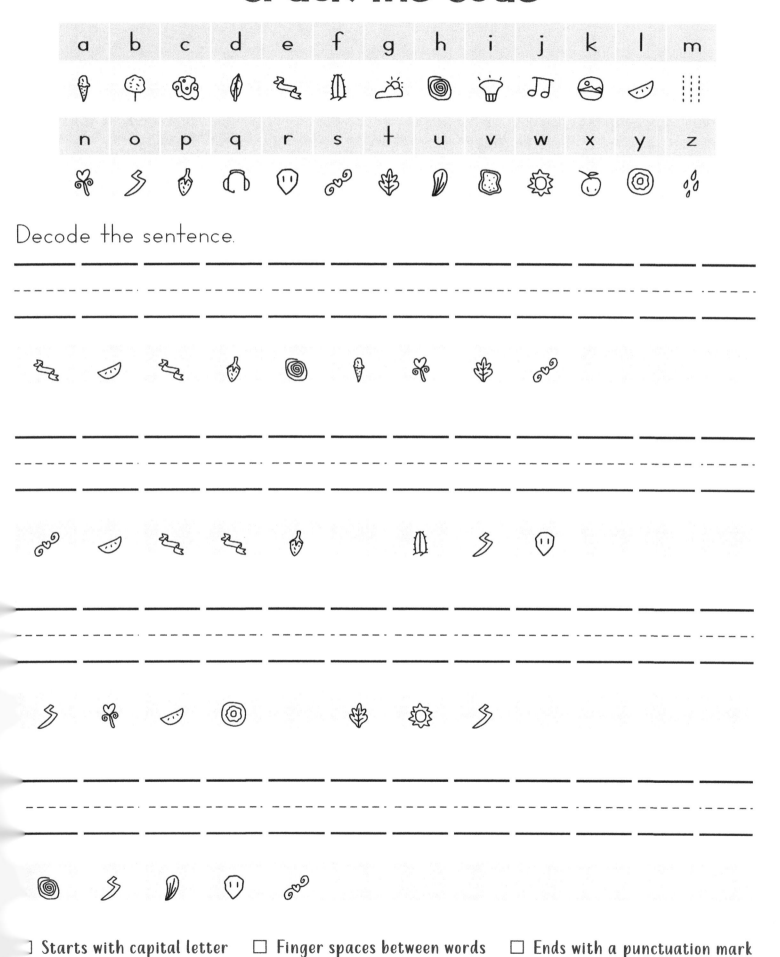

Certificate

Congratulations! You've finished Handwriting Practice Made Fun: Jokes, Riddles, Stories, and More! You did a great job. Visit our website for a downloadable certificate to celebrate your achievement. Keep up the good work!

Made in the USA
Middletown, DE
06 January 2023

21502783R00073